CLOTHES & CRAFTS IN THE
MIDDLE AGES

Imogen Dawson

DILLON PRESS
Parsippany, New Jersey

A ZOË BOOK

© 1997 Zoë Books Limited

Devised and produced by
Zoë Books Limited
15 Worthy Lane
Winchester
Hampshire SO23 7AB
England

First published in Great Britain in 1997 by
Zoë Books Limited
15 Worthy Lane
Winchester
Hampshire SO23 7AB

Printed in Belgium by Proost N.V.
Editor: Kath Davies
Design & Production: Sterling Associates
Illustrations: Virginia Gray

Published in the United States in 1998 by
 Dillon Press
A Division of Simon & Schuster
299 Jefferson Road
Parsippany, New Jersey 07054-0480

Library of Congress Cataloging-in-Publication Data

Dawson, Imogen
    Clothes & crafts in the Middle Ages / Imogen Dawson.
        p. cm.
    Includes index.
    Summary: Describe clothes and crafts throughout the
Middle Ages in Europe while also discussing the
everyday life of the people, their technological skills,
and social and economic systems.
        1. Handicraft—Europe—History—Juvenile literature.
    2. Clothing and dress—History—Juvenile literature.
    3. Civilization, Medieval—Juvenile literature.
    4. Middle Ages—History—Juvenile literature.
    5. Europe—History—476-1492—Juvenile literature.
    [1. Handicraft—Europe. 2. Clothing and dress—History
    3. Civilization, Medieval. 4. Middle Ages—History.
    5. Europe—History—476-1492.] I. Title.
    TT55.D38 1998
    940.1—dc21   97-8326
                                                          CIP
                                                          AC

ISBN 0-382-39699-5 (LSB)   10 9 8 7 6 5 4 3 2 1
ISBN 0-382-39700-2 (PBK)   10 9 8 7 6 5 4 3 2 1

Author's note

The period that historians call the Middle Ages
overlaps with the period known as the Renaissance.
For a greater understanding of historical continuity
and development, some examples and references to
crafts, clothes, and festivals in this book fall outside
the period that historians define as the Middle Ages
and may, strictly speaking, be considered Renaissance.

Photographic acknowledgments

The publishers wish to acknowledge, with thanks,
the following photographic sources:

DDA Photo Library / Thyssen-Bornemisza Museum,
Madrid 19br; C.M Dixon 14, 15b / The British
Library 9t/ The British Museum, London 13tr /
Victoria & Albert Museum, London 17t, 19bl, 21t /
Künsthistorisches Museum, Vienna 20t / Palazzo
Vecchio, Florence 22t; e.t.archive 11tl, 15t, 17b, 25t
& b / Prado Museum, Madrid title page, 7tl, 10t /
Victoria & Albert Museum, London 3, 8b, 21b /
Royal Chapel, Granada 4t / Hamburg Staatsarchiv
5t / The Louvre, Paris 5b / The British Library,
London 6t / Torre Aquila Trento 6b, 16t & bl, 18c /
University Library, Heidelberg 7tr, 24t / Biblioteca
Estense, Modena 7b, 18b, 24b / Correr Museum,
Venice 8t / Musée de Cluny, Paris 9b / Suermondt
Museum, Aachen 10b / Museo delgi Argenti, Pitti
Palace, Florence 11tc / Real Collegiata San Isidoro,
Leon 11b / Bibliotheque Nationale, Paris 12t /
Archaeological Museum Cividale Friuli 13tl /
Palazzo Pubblico, Siena 16br / Musée Conde
Chantilly 18t / British Museum, London 19t /
Bargello Museum, Florence 20b / Stadtmuseum
Trier (Salomon Collection) 22b / Palazzo Giuntini di
Valfonda/Venturi 23t / Sir John Soane's Museum,
London 23b; Mansell Collection 13b; Tony Morrison
12b.

Cover: e.t.archive / Bargello Museum, Florence, top
right / Diocesan Museum, Mantua, top left /
Biblioteca Estense, Modena, bottom left; C.M.Dixon
/ Victoria & Albert Museum, London, center; DDA
Photo Library / Thyssen-Bornemisza Museum,
Madrid, bottom right.

The publishers have made every effort to trace the
copyright holders, but if they have inadvertently
overlooked any, they will be pleased to make the
necessary arrangement at the first opportunity.

CONTENTS

INTRODUCTION

The period of history in Europe that we call the Middle Ages lasted for more than 1,000 years, from the collapse of the Roman Empire in A.D. 476. Before Christopher Columbus arrived in America in 1492, Europeans believed that the world stretched only from Western Europe to India and China in the East.

There were far fewer people living in Europe in the Middle Ages than there are today. Most people lived in the countryside and worked on the land. People made their clothes and crafts from local materials such as wool, leather, wood, clay, and iron.

Most people followed the **Christian** religion. The Church was very rich and powerful in the Middle Ages. The head of

▲ King Ferdinand and Queen Isabella of Spain were rich and powerful rulers. They paid for Christopher Columbus's voyages to America. The gold and craft goods he brought back were claimed by them.

The Black Death

In the 1300s about a third of all people in Europe died from a disease called the plague, or the **Black Death**.

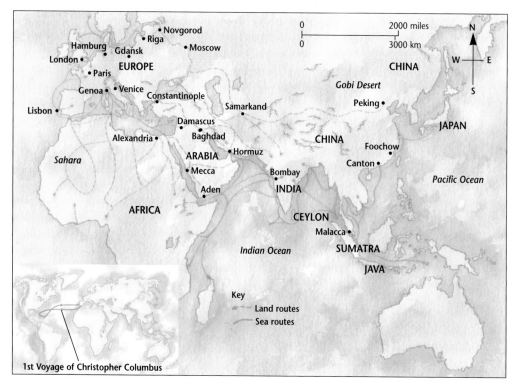

1st Voyage of Christopher Columbus

◀ Traders, or **merchants**, traveled great distances to buy and sell goods. They sailed along the rivers of Europe, or around its coast, and later to North and South America. Some merchants traveled overland to India and China. They brought back goods such as **silk** and **spices**. They carried the goods on pack animals such as donkeys and camels.

paid craft workers to make new works in these styles. A rebirth of ideas from ancient Greece and Rome occurred at this time.

▲ This drawing of the port of Hamburg in Germany was made in 1497. Hamburg was a busy trading city. You can see the merchants dressed in rich clothes, watching their ships being loaded with goods.

The Crusades

Between the end of the 1000s and the 1300s, large groups of **knights** and nobles traveled from Europe to the Middle East. They took soldiers with them to fight for the Christian holy places, such as Jerusalem in Palestine. These journeys were called the **Crusades**. The Christian rulers in Western Europe thought that the Turks, who followed the religion of **Islam**, should not control the Christian Holy Land.

the Church, the **Pope**, made the religious laws, which everyone, including rulers, had to obey. Rich **nobles** and merchants gave land and money to the Church. Craft workers were paid to make works of art for churches and cathedrals.

Written records, such as the books and maps made by **monks** and **nuns**, give us information about the Middle Ages. Paintings and drawings from that time show us how people lived and worked and the kinds of clothes that they wore.

The time at the end of the Middle Ages is called the **Renaissance**, which means "rebirth." People became interested in the writings, buildings, paintings, and sculptures of ancient Greece and Rome. Rich people brought back ancient works of art from their travels in Europe. They

▼ This detail, from a painting by Frans Francken, shows a range of craft goods. Only the rich could afford to buy such items, which were made by highly skilled craft workers.

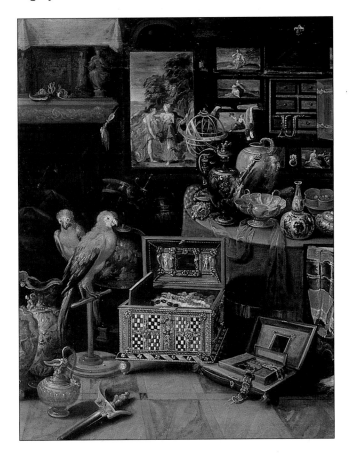

CRAFTS

Most people lived very simply during the Middle Ages. Everyday things were made from local materials. Only rich people could afford to buy materials and craft goods that came from far away.

People used wood and stone to build their houses and to make furniture. They made jugs and bowls from clay. The **blacksmith** made farm tools, weapons, and cooking tools, or utensils, from iron.

Wood

During the Middle Ages forests covered most of Europe. People used wood for building and to make boats, carts, and furniture such as benches, tables, and chests. Rich nobles, who lived in castles or **manor** houses, often decorated the walls

The feudal system

During the Middle Ages the rulers of countries in Europe gave nobles, or lords, the rights, or feus, to land. In return the lords promised to support the ruler and to provide soldiers who would fight for the ruler in battle.

The **peasants** who lived and worked on the land grew food and raised animals. They had to give some of their food to the nobles who owned the land. Many peasants were not free to move to another part of the country. They were "tied'" to the land.

of their homes with wooden panels. In France and in Scotland, craft workers painted bright pictures on wooden ceiling panels.

Most homes contained a table, benches, beds, and chests and perhaps some stools made of wood. The chest was the most useful piece of furniture. It could be used as a seat, a table, a sideboard, or to store things.

Some nobles slept in four-poster beds. These had four carved posts to hold up a frame. Curtains made of heavy material hung from the frame.

◀ This Italian wall painting, or **fresco**, shows life at a manor house in the summer. Many things, including some of the buildings and tools, are made of wood.

▲ There is very little furniture in this room–just a wooden chest and a chair. This picture was painted by Hieronymus Bosch about 1500.

▶ People in the Middle Ages loved board games. Chess, which is still played today, was very popular. This drawing, made in 1381, comes from a German manuscript. The ruler, Otto IV, is playing a game of chess.

Nobles traveled around to oversee their lands or to follow the **court**. They took furniture and their most valuable possessions with them. These objects had to be made so that they could be carried easily. Craft workers made chairs and stools that folded up, boxes for jewelry, and chests with strong locks and handles for clothes.

Courts

The court was a gathering of noble lords and ladies and was held wherever the ruler was staying at the time. There were grand feasts at court. The nobles were entertained by singers and musicians, jugglers, poets, and storytellers.

◀ Nobles enjoy music and dancing at court in the summer. The ruler sits in the chair on the left.

Cloth

The wool trade was very important in the Middle Ages. Selling wool and woolen cloth brought wealth to merchants and sheep farmers, including many **monasteries**. Some of the most expensive wool came from the Cotswolds area of England. Merchants sold the wool as far away as Italy.

Turning wool into cloth was a long process. Women worked at home, spinning the wool into long thread, using a **spindle** and a **distaff**. They wove the thread into woolen cloth on a **loom**. Then the cloth had to be washed before it was dyed into different colors. People used all kinds of plants and mosses to dye the wool.

Women in poorer families wove cloth for everyday purposes such as clothes and blankets. Women in richer households and in **convents** also embroidered or wove tapestries.

▲ These merchants in Venice, Italy, are weighing wool in a basket. The drawing was made in 1380.

◄ This woman spins wool while she is out in the fields. She holds the distaff under her arm and the spindle in her other hand. The drawing was made in France during the late fifteenth century.

▲ This picture, drawn in the late fourteenth century, shows a tapestry being woven on a wooden frame. You can see the crisscross threads. The weavers often worked from a sketch made by an artist, which was called a cartoon.

Carpets and tapestries

Unlike today the word *carpet* was used for all kinds of woven covers and hangings, not just for floor coverings.

The word *tapestry* comes from the French word *tapis*, or "carpet."

People used carpets to cover walls, to keep out drafts, or to divide rooms.

Some nobles took their carpets and tapestries on their travels. They were easy to roll up and carry around.

Linen

Linen cloth is made from the long, tough stems of a plant called flax. In the Middle Ages, people softened the flax by leaving it to rot for a time. This was called retting. Then they beat the flax with wooden paddles, so that the stems separated into **fibers**. This was very hard work. The strong fibers were spun into linen cloth. If the flax fibers were thin, the cloth was very fine, and if the fibers were thicker, the linen was coarse. Fine linen was very expensive.

▼ This is one of a set of beautiful tapestries known as *The Lady and the Unicorn*. The tapestries were made in France during the fifteenth century.

From kitchen to table

Kitchen utensils were probably hung from hooks on the kitchen walls. There was usually little furniture in a kitchen, except for a large table and perhaps a wooden chopping block for meat.

Kitchen utensils

The records of a rich merchant in the 1300s list his kitchen utensils:

"...1 great brass bowl; 2 great copper jars for water; 2 iron pots, that hung on a chain above the fire; 1 copper frying pan; 4 other frying pans, 2 spits and a grill; 20 oil-jars; 1 copper pan 'for making black pudding'; 1 big pan for melting lard [animal fat]; 1 sieve and an iron shovel 'for making pills'; 1 sugar barrel; 1 salt box."

▲ The most elaborate tableware, made of silver and gold, was used at feasts for the rich. This detail is from a painting by two Flemish artists.

In the early Middle Ages, people ate from wooden bowls or platters. They also used slabs of stale bread, called trenchers, as plates. Later on, people used pottery and metal dishes and plates. Pottery was made locally and sold in the markets. In northern Europe a grey metal called pewter was used to make plates, jugs, and dishes.

Pewter is a mixture of tin and small amounts of lead and copper. The pewterer poured the hot metal into **molds**. When it cooled, it was polished until it shone like silver. Jugs, or flagons, were made in separate pieces. The pewterer joined, or

◀ You can see, the grey pewter dishes and jugs, as well as pottery on the table in this picture. This painting of *The Last Supper* is by the Dutch artist Lucas van Leyden.

▲ During the Middle Ages more coins were made, or **minted**, and began to be widely used. Before this time people had exchanged, or bartered, goods. Local rulers had the right to produce their own coins. This coin was minted for the government in Genoa, Italy.

◀ Pope Clement VII gave this cup to a church in Florence, Italy. It was carved from a piece of precious stone called jasper.

Very wealthy people owned gold plates and drinking cups or goblets. Sometimes the tableware was decorated with precious stones, or jewels.

The search for gold

In Europe the demand for gold to make coins, jewelry, and crafts of all kinds was increasing. After Columbus reached America, the search for gold led explorers farther into the lands of the Americas. The traders, who were mostly Spanish, melted down local craft goods made of gold. Then they sent the gold blocks back to Europe.

soldered, the pieces together with hot, melted metal. This made a bridge between the pieces, which held them together after the metal cooled and hardened. The best pewterers were so skilled that you could not see the joins. Pewter was cheaper to buy than silver, so it was called poor man's silver.

Fine glass and silver were made in France and in Venice and other parts of Italy. The richer the family, the finer its tableware.

▶ Boxes called reliquaries were specially made for the Church. They held the remains of a saint or other holy objects. This reliquary is crafted from gold and enamel. It was made in Spain during the thirteenth century.

Towns and cities

Towns and cities grew in size during the Middle Ages. They were important centers for trade, and they also became centers of learning.

Craft workers such as candlemakers, jewelers, and glovemakers made goods in their town workshops. They sold the goods from the front of the workshop or on market stalls. Potters and leather workers needed more room for their crafts, so they often worked near the edge of the towns.

Merchants grew more powerful as their trade increased. Nobles and merchants were now able to order and buy crafts that were made for their beauty rather than for everyday use. Life was still hard for poor people. In towns a whole family might live in one room of a house.

◀ Students attend a class at the Sorbonne University in Paris, France, during the sixteenth century.

After the Black Death swept across Europe in the fourteenth century, the craft workers who did survive were in even greater demand.

One of the earliest and most famous universities in Europe was founded in the city of Bologna, Italy, during the eleventh century. At first universities were places where men studied to become priests, lawyers, or doctors.

▲ Many towns still have a guildhall, where guild members once met. This one is in Lavenham, England, which was formerly a rich wool town.

Craft guilds

In the Middle Ages, craft **guilds** were set up in each town. A guild was an organization that made sure that its members were properly trained as **apprentices** and produced high-quality goods.

An apprentice spent seven years learning a trade. Boys could become apprentices in most places. In some places girls were apprentices as well, but only in certain trades. Their parents paid for them to live at the home of the craft worker who taught them their skills.

At the end of the seven-year apprenticeship, they had to make a special piece called a masterpiece, to show that they were good enough to join the craft guild.

Guilds also set a fair price for their goods. There was a guild for each type of craft, such as goldsmiths or shoemakers.

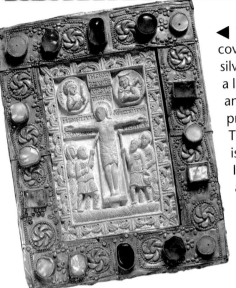

◀ This book cover is made of silver, **gilded** with a layer of gold and set with precious stones. The center panel is carved ivory. It was made for an Italian noble in the eighth century.

▲ These highly decorated pages are from an illuminated manuscript made in Paris early in the fifteenth century.

Books

Books were written, copied, and bound by hand, usually in monasteries or convents. Sometimes it took years to produce one book. Many of these **manuscripts** had brightly colored pictures of people, animals, and flowers and had gold decoration. Often these pictures formed part of the first letter in each section of a book. Manuscripts decorated in this way are called **illuminated** manuscripts.

When moveable-type printing was invented in the fifteenth century, there were many more books for people to buy and to study. We know that books were precious at this time, because they were mentioned in people's wills. Books were very expensive and beyond the reach of poorer people, who in any case could not read.

William Caxton

William Caxton was an English wool merchant who learned the craft of printing in Germany. In 1476, he set up the first printing press in England. He printed and published all kinds of books in English, from poetry to an illustrated encyclopedia. Caxton also translated histories and religious works into English. On the right is a page from one of his translations, *The lives of the fathers*. It was printed by his assistant in 1495, shortly after Caxton's death.

Important buildings

During the Middle Ages many of the best craft workers traveled around Europe to work on important buildings. Palaces and cathedrals were being built from stone and marble. Craft workers decorated them with stone or wooden carvings, stained glass, and painted pillars and ceilings.

▲ This splendid stained-glass window at Canterbury Cathedral portrays Henry VIII, who became King of England in 1509.

The "Prentice Pillar"

The "Prentice Pillar" is in Rosslyn Chapel, near Edinburgh, Scotland. The chapel was built around 1450. This is the story that is told about it.

An apprentice was given permission to carve the pillar while the master mason was away. When the master returned, he saw that the pillar was so beautifully carved that it outshone all his own work. In a rage the master hit the apprentice over the head so hard that he killed him. The master was hanged for the murder of the apprentice.

Rich nobles employed craft workers to decorate their homes with paintings, sculptures, and frescoes. In Spain, people put brightly colored pottery tiles on their floors and walls.

Spanish crafts were influenced by the styles of the **Moors**. These people came from North Africa and ruled part of Spain in the early Middle Ages. They were followers of Islam.

Metalwork

Craft workers used many different metals and ways of working to decorate houses and churches. Patterns in iron, called wrought iron, decorated doors and chests. Bronze was popular for candlesticks and crosses in churches and was sometimes used to make larger objects such as doors.

Some craft workers were skilled at gilding paintings, sculptures, and carvings.

▲ An Italian sculptor, Lorenzo Ghiberti, made these huge bronze doors for the Baptistery in Florence. The sculptures on the doors show scenes from the Bible. They took almost 50 years to make and were finished in 1452.

Frescoes

Frescoes are pictures painted directly onto wet plaster. As the plaster on the wall or ceiling dries, the paint sets into clear, bright colors. Italian artists created some of the most beautiful frescoes, which can still be seen in churches and public buildings in Italy.

Mosaics

Thousands of tiny pieces of colored stones or tiles make up patterns and pictures called mosaics. They were often used to decorate houses and churches.

The mosaics in St. Mark's Cathedral, Venice, cover the floors, walls, and ceilings. They took more than 200 years to complete.

▶ These tiles and carvings are in the Alhambra, a palace built by the Moors near Granada in Spain. The carved writing is in Arabic, the language of the Moors and other peoples from North Africa.

CLOTHES AND JEWELRY

Workers' clothes were simple in shape and style. Women and girls wore a shapeless dress, or **kirtle**, with wide sleeves. Men and boys wore leggings or trousers and a smock or tunic. The materials were mostly wool and linen.

Both women and men wore hoods and capes or lengths of material wrapped around them in cold weather. Adults often cut down their old clothes to make clothes for children.

Fashions changed slowly, and only rich people could afford to follow them. As travelers brought news of different styles, wealthy people began to wear more fitted clothes. Women's dresses had tight sleeves and bodices, and sometimes women wore a sleeveless coat, called a surcoat, over them. Long trains trailing behind the dresses were also fashionable.

▲ This is part of a fresco painted about 1400. You can see the workers harvesting corn. The women are wearing kirtles, while the men wear smocks and leggings.

The clothes that people wore in the Middle Ages were very different from the clothes that we wear today. The materials were much coarser, and there were fewer colors.

▼ A detail from a fresco of Siena, Italy, shows how nobles and their servants dressed in the early fourteenth century.

▲ These nobles are out riding, about 1400. The women are riding sidesaddle because of their long dresses.

In the later Middle Ages, women's dresses had wide, stiff sleeves and a stiff, starched collar, or ruff. Men wore ruffs, too. Their jackets and short trousers were padded and embroidered. Women supported their wide skirts with padding called a farthingale. Men and women wore colored silks and velvets.

Headdresses

By the 1400s, women wore stiff, shaped headdresses instead of the simple veils of earlier times. In Italy jeweled caps were popular, and bands that kept women's plaited hair in place. In France, women covered their hair with a cloth called a wimple, which fastened under the chin. Noblewomen wore a cone-shaped hat with a veil, called a hennin. Men wore caps or hats with feathers and jewels in them.

▲ Nobles wore rich, brightly colored clothes and elaborate hats and caps when they went hunting. This detail is from a French tapestry made about 1440.

Laws about dress

Noble people wore fine clothes and jewelry to show their rank. When many merchants became rich as a result of increasing trade, they showed their new wealth by wearing clothes like the nobles.

The nobles thought that this was a threat to their position. They passed laws to keep the merchants from dressing in the same style as the nobles. However, many people ignored the laws.

◀ This print shows William Caxton presenting a book to the Queen of England about 1477. She and the noblewomen of the court are wearing hennin headdresses. The long pointed shoes were very fashionable. The shoes were called crackowes because the style came from Kraków in Poland.

Fashions for men and boys

During the 1300s rich men wore a short, tight-fitting tunic under a long-sleeved coat, or cotehardie. Sometimes the cotehardie had a badge or pattern on it, and later on the sleeves were cut in a zigzag, or jagged, shape. The coat might be trimmed with fur or made of expensive material such as silk or **damask**.

Men and boys also wore brightly colored garments, called hose. Sometimes there was a different color for each leg!

Around the beginning of the 1500s, men's fashions changed. Wealthy men now wore short, padded tunics, or doublets, with a waistcoat and a fur-lined longcoat. Soon elaborate puffed sleeves were worn, which could be removed.

▲ These wealthy French nobles are wearing clothes made from expensive fabrics, richly embroidered with gold. Some are wearing fur hats. The picture comes from an illuminated manuscript made early in the fifteenth century.

▶ This farm worker is wearing simply shaped clothes, with no decoration. They are made from coarse, tough cloth. Peasants did not follow fashion. Their style of clothes stayed the same for hundreds of years.

◀ In this detail from a fifteenth century manuscript, Italian merchants, traders, and shopkeepers wear cotehardies. The customer on the left wears a short tunic and brightly colored hose.

▲ King Henry VIII of England is wearing a style of hat that became very fashionable in the 1500s. His padded tunic and long coat are richly decorated with gold thread. Will Sommers, Henry's jester, is wearing much plainer clothes.

The special clothes and hats that town mayors wear in England today are very like the styles of the 1500s.

◀ Nicholas Hilliard painted many miniatures of English nobles. This portrait of a young man shows his embroidered cloak, and short jeweled doublet. He wears a lace ruff around his neck.

Armor

In the 1100s, knights wore metal helmets and **chain mail** in battle. However, chain mail could not protect the knight completely from weapons such as arrows. The armorers, who were very skilled craft workers, began to invent new types of armor.

The new armor was made of very strong iron and steel. There were metal plates that fit around the knight's body and were held in place with leather straps.

▲ The Italian Vittore Carpaccio painted this picture in 1510. The young knight in the foreground is wearing full body armor.

Jewelry

Nobles and other wealthy people wore jewelry to show how rich and important they were. Men and women wore earrings, rings, brooches, and necklaces made of gold and often set with many jewels. Wealthy people also had precious stones embroidered into their clothes and hats.

As with other crafts, styles of jewelry changed over time. In the later Middle Ages, gold jewelry from Florence, Italy, became very popular. Many goldsmiths had workshops on a bridge over the Arno River, in the middle of Florence. Today jewelry is sold from shops on the same bridge.

▼ The head in the middle of this gold brooch was carved from a precious stone that had two layers. The brown layer has been carved to show a little of the white layer. This kind of carving is called a cameo. It was made in Italy during the fourteenth century.

▲ Maria de' Medici came from one of the richest and most powerful families in Italy. This portrait of her as a young girl was painted by Allori. The painting shows her wealth–the gold jewelry, the pearls, and the richly embroidered clothes. Later, Maria became Queen of France.

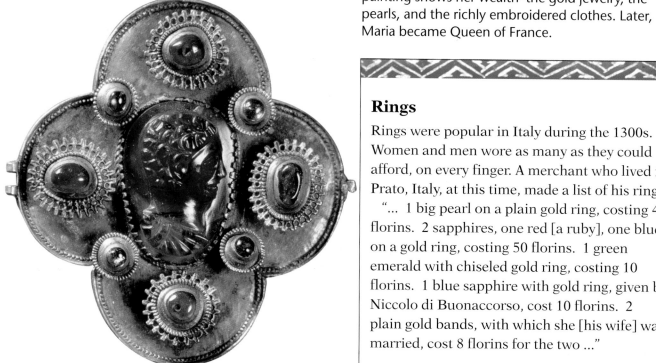

Rings

Rings were popular in Italy during the 1300s. Women and men wore as many as they could afford, on every finger. A merchant who lived in Prato, Italy, at this time, made a list of his rings:

"... 1 big pearl on a plain gold ring, costing 40 florins. 2 sapphires, one red [a ruby], one blue, on a gold ring, costing 50 florins. 1 green emerald with chiseled gold ring, costing 10 florins. 1 blue sapphire with gold ring, given by Niccolo di Buonaccorso, cost 10 florins. 2 plain gold bands, with which she [his wife] was married, cost 8 florins for the two ..."

Heraldry

From the 1100s onward, knights decorated their shields with strong patterns in bright colors. These **heraldic designs** helped soldiers to recognize friends and enemies across a battlefield.

The designs were also called coats of arms because the knights wore them on their surcoats. This sleeveless overcoat or cloak protected the knight's armor.

The coat of arms was also embroidered on a small flag called a pennon, which flew from the knight's lance.

▲ Queen Elizabeth I of England wore magnificent jewelry and dresses. This miniature of her was painted by Nicholas Hilliard.

▶ Crosses, stripes, lions, diamonds, flowers, and crescents were among the heraldic designs to be seen at the battle between France and England at Agincourt in the fifteenth century.

FESTIVALS AND HOLIDAYS

Craft workers had to work very long hours. They began work at dawn and finished at nightfall. However, there were holidays and festivals throughout the year when very few people worked. Most festivals were religious, but some were held to celebrate special events, such as the marriage of a ruler.

Special days

There were about 50 special religious or holy days on which people did not work. There were three types of holy days. The first was Sunday, when nobody worked. The second was for everyone except those

▲ Musicians play woodwind instruments while young people hold hands and dance in the street. This detail comes from an Italian tapestry.

who were plowing the fields. On a third type of holy day, all work was done except housework!

▶ The Flemish artist, Pieter Bruegel painted this picture called *A Country Feast and Dancing* in the sixteenth century. He came from a family of artists who liked to paint ordinary people.

The ways in which people celebrated festivals changed very little over hundreds of years. In the sixteenth century the opportunity to eat plenty of food and to dance were still the most enjoyable parts of a festival for country people.

Mystery plays

In the 1300s and 1400s, craft workers in many towns in Europe performed **mystery plays** for special occasions. Each craft guild acted out a different story from the Bible. Often the guild chose a story to link with its own trade. In York the shipbuilders chose the story of Noah and his boat, or ark.

The players used carts or wagons in the marketplace for a stage. Usually the plays were performed on a holy day in the summer. In some towns the best play won a prize.

▲ This fresco shows a festival in a palace garden at Valfonda, Italy. The festival was held to celebrate the marriage of Maria de' Medici to King Henry IV of France.

Pilgrimages

In the Middle Ages many people traveled to holy places, or **shrines**. These were places where saints had lived or where **miracles** had happened. Sick people hoped that they might get well if they visited shrines. Someone who made a special journey like this was called a pilgrim, and the journey was called a pilgrimage.

Some pilgrims traveled across Europe to Tours in France, to Santiago de Compostela in Spain, or to Rome in Italy. Although the journeys were for serious purposes, for many pilgrims they were holidays as well.

Monks always wore special clothes. Their long gown, called a habit, was tied with a simple rope belt, and they wore a hooded cloak. They shaved the hair from the top of their head, in a style called a tonsure.

Sometimes monks who went on pilgrimages wore very uncomfortable clothes and no shoes. They did this to show they were sorry, or repented, for the wrong things they had done.

◄ These pages from an illuminated manuscript made about 1500 show monks on their way to St. Peter's Church in Rome.

The Age of Chivalry

The time from about 1000 to 1400 was called the Age of Chivalry. Knights were called *chevalerie* from a French word meaning a horseman. It was a great honor to become a knight. After a long training period, a young nobleman had to show that he was honest and honorable. He swore to do his duty and to serve his lord and his ruler faithfully.

Tournaments

In order to encourage the knights and to give them some practice in the skills of fighting, lords held meetings, or tournaments, where knights gathered to show their skills. They fought in mock battles and in one-to-one, single combat. The ladies of the court presented prizes to the winners.

The knights used their lances in contests called jousting. Sometimes knights were hurt or even killed in these tournaments.

▲ Prince Henry of Breslau has just won the tournament. He is presented a prize by the ladies of the court. The drawing comes from an early fourteenth century manuscript made in Germany.

▼ This drawing from an Italian **medieval** Bible shows knights jousting at a tournament.

▲ Trumpeters play from the minstrel's gallery, while the lady of the manor and her guests are served their dinner.

Feasts

A feast at a castle or manor house was a great occasion. Perhaps the lord had returned from a crusade, or the ruler was visiting. All the guests wore their very best clothes and jewels. They were entertained as they ate an enormous meal. Sometimes there were jugglers and acrobats, or there was a play to watch. Also at feasts were music and dancing.

Minstrels and troubadours

Musicians, or minstrels, traveled around the country, playing at special feasts and other events. These minstrels were very skilled. They played horns and trumpets, harps and **lutes**. They sang stories in songs called ballads.

Poems about adventures and about love were very popular at the courts in

France, Italy, and Spain between the 1100s and the 1300s. Young poets called troubadours entertained the nobles with these long poems and sang love songs. Often the troubadours were also princes or nobles.

The King's minstrel

Great lords and rulers sometimes kept a group, or troupe, of minstrels who were especially skilled. One story is told about a famous minstrel called Blondel. An English king was imprisoned in a castle somewhere in Austria. Blondel wandered around the outside of many castles, singing a special song that he and the king had made up together. One day he heard the song being sung from inside a castle, in reply to him. Blondel knew that, at last, he had found the king.

▼ Adenet, "king of the minstrels," entertains two noble ladies in this drawing from a French thirteenth century manuscript.

Dressing in the medieval style

Most people dressed very simply in the Middle Ages. Children wore the same style of clothes as their parents. Girls wore a dress, or kirtle. Boys wore a tunic, or gownlike garment, and leggings.

You will need: • one sheet or large piece of material • a scarf • tights or trousers.

To make a kirtle:

1.   Cut a hole in the middle of the material. Make it just large enough to fit your head through.

2.   Put the material over your head.

3.   Tie the scarf around your waist to make a belt.

To make a tunic:

1.   Cut a strip off the material or sheet, about as wide as your shoulders and about as long as your height.

2.   Cut a hole in the middle of the strip of material. Make it just large enough to fit your head through.

3.   Put the cloth over your head so that it covers your front and back.

4.   Tie the scarf around your waist to make a belt.

5.   Put on the tights or trousers.

Jewelry

Most poor people had no decorations on their clothes. Rich people wore lots of jewelry to show their wealth and importance. Make a chain for yourself.

You will need: • paper • aluminum foil • glue.

1. Glue aluminum foil to each side of a piece of paper, covering the whole piece. Cut it into narrow strips about three inches long.

2. Glue the ends of one strip together to make a link.

3. Thread another strip through the first link and glue the ends together to make a second link.

4. Continue adding links until your chain is long enough to go around your neck and as far as your chest.

Medieval entertainers

Form a group with friends to put on a show in medieval style, or entertain your family and friends by yourself. Dress in the medieval costume you have made. Here are some of the things you could do.

1. Choose a poem you like or make one up. Learn it by heart and practice saying it aloud. You could choose some music, played on a stringed instrument, to accompany your poem.

2. Put on a variety show. Ask each friend with a special skill to practice for a performance that will last for only a few minutes. You could have a juggler, a singer, a joke teller or jester, a musician, a poet or storyteller, and dancers. Make sure that each performance is different and that it doesn't last too long. Choose the order for the entertainers and practice introducing them before you put on the show.

3. Choose some music that you or your friends can play on woodwind, brass, or stringed instruments. If you choose music with a strong rhythm, you could dance to the music as well.

A coat of arms

Noble families had their own coat of arms. The royal family of England had a design with a lion on it. The French nobles wore a flower design called a *fleur-de-lis*. The crusaders wore a cross on their tunics, to show that they were fighting for the Church.

You could make your own coat of arms. Choose your favorite colors or patterns when you design your coat of arms. You could draw something that you like or that is important to you, as well as a pattern.

You will need: • poster paper or cardboard • coloring pens or paint • scissors • sealing tape.

1. Draw your design on the poster paper or cardboard and color it in.

2. When the design is dry, cut it out.

3. Stick it onto your clothes with tape.

A pilgrim's badge

Pilgrims also wore special badges to show that they were on a pilgrimage. The pilgrims who traveled to Santiago de Compostela in Spain, to the shrine of St. James, had a badge that looked like a small scallop shell. It was made of clay or pewter. This scallop is still called a *coquille de Saint-Jacques*, or "St. James's shell."

You will need: • modeling clay • paint • safety pin or bar pin • tape or glue.

1. Make the clay into the shape of a shell or any other shape you like. Make it quite thin, so that it isn't too heavy.

2. When the clay has hardened, paint your badge.

3. When the paint is dry, tape or glue the pin to the back of the badge. Now your badge is ready to wear.

An illuminated manuscript

You can make your own illuminated manuscript like those the monks and nuns made in the Middle Ages. Remember that they often drew pictures that showed the people and animals in the story or poem.

You will need: • a pencil • coloring pencils or pens • a ruler • a gold pen • a black writing pen • paper.

1. Find a poem or short story that you like. You could make up your own or copy something from a book.

2. Use a ruler to measure a margin about $^3/_4$ or 1 inch inside the edges of the paper. This will make a frame so that you can write inside this area.

3. Draw the frame in gold.

4. Use your pencil to sketch how things will fit inside the frame. Allow space for a big box at the beginning of your poem or story. This is for the first letter of the first word.

5. When you are happy with your sketch, draw the box with a gold pen. Also in gold, write the first letter, very big, inside the box.

6. Use your colored pens to draw patterns or a picture inside the box around the letter.

7. Write the rest of the poem or story with a black writing pen. Then with friends or family sit around your own round table, like King Arthur and his knights, and share your poems and stories.

GLOSSARY

apprentice: Someone who is learning a trade.

Black Death: A plague that killed about 25 million people in Europe in the 1300s. It was spread by fleas on rats.

blacksmith: A blacksmith used hot iron to make and mend all types of tools and weapons. The iron was heated in a very hot fire and then shaped on a metal block, called an anvil. As the iron cooled, it set hard.

chain mail: Armor made of linked rings, or chains, of metal.

Christian: A follower of the teachings of Jesus Christ.

convent: The place where nuns live and work. In the Middle Ages some convents were governed by an abbot or an abbess and were called abbeys. They often included a church and farmland.

court: A gathering of a ruler and nobles, or the place where they met.

Crusades: Journeys to fight the Muslims for possession of the Holy Land. There were six major Crusades between 1095 and 1291.

damask: Cloth that has a woven pattern, first made in Damascus in Syria.

distaff: A stick that holds wool or flax for spinning.

fibers: Strong, threadlike parts of a plant.

frescoes: Pictures painted onto damp plaster.

gilding: Putting a thin layer of gold onto something.

guilds: Organizations of workers in the same craft or trade.

heraldic designs: The special patterns that make up a coat of arms.

illuminated: Decorated or illustrated with patterns and pictures.

Islam: A religion started by Muhammad in 622. Its followers are called Muslims.

kirtle: A long, loose gown. Later, an outer petticoat.

knights: Soldiers on horseback who fought for a ruler. Horses and armor were expensive, so knighthood became an honor for rich men.

loom: A wooden frame for weaving cloth.

lute: A musical instrument with strings.

manor: The land belonging to a noble family.

manuscripts: Books written by hand, usually done before printing was invented. The word comes from two Latin words—*manus* which means hand and *scriptus* which means "written."

medieval: From the Middle Ages.

merchants: Traders, people who buy and sell goods.

minted: Made (money). The place where coins are made is called a mint.

miracle: An event that cannot be explained by scientific laws.

molds: Hollow forms that shape materials such as clay, plaster, metal, or glass.

monastery: The place where monks live and work. In the Middle Ages some monasteries had large amounts of land, which the monks farmed.

monks: Men who give their lives to serving God. They pray and hold several church services every day. In the Middle Ages they were teachers and farmers. Monks do not marry.

Moors: People who lived in north-western Africa. They ruled Spain from 711-1492.

mystery play: Plays, sometimes called miracle plays, that told stories from the Bible. Also includes stories that cannot be explained.

nobles: The most important people in a country, after the ruler's family. They held important positions at court and were usually very rich.

nuns: Women who give their lives to serving God and who do not marry. In the Middle Ages, nuns taught, farmed, and made tapestries.

peasants: Land workers.

Pope: In the early Middle Ages, there was one Christian Church. It was called "catholic," which means general or universal. The Pope, who lived mostly in Rome, was the head of the Church. Later other churches were formed. Today the Pope heads the Roman Catholic Church.

Renaissance: The time from about 1400 to about 1600 when people's interest in the ideas, art, and architecture of ancient Greece and Rome was "reborn."

shrines: Places where people remember holy people or saints.

silk: A thread made by silkworm caterpillars that is woven into soft cloth.

spices: Dried plant seeds, roots, or leaves, such as ginger, pepper, and nutmeg, used to flavor foods. Spices were very expensive during the Middle Ages.

spindle: A pin or rod, usually made from wood, which turns or winds thread when it is being spun.

Further Reading

Corbishly, Mike. *Middle Ages*. New York: Facts on File, 1990.

Cox, Reg, and Neil Morris. *The Seven Wonders of the Historic World* (The Wonders of the World series). Parsippany, N.J.: Silver Burdett Press, 1996.

Dawson, Imogen. *In the Middle Ages* (Food & Feasts series). Parsippany, N.J.: Silver Burdett Press, 1994.

Macdonald, Fiona. *Marco Polo* (The World in the Time of series). Parsippany, N.J.: Silver Burdett Press, 1997.

Paul, Penelope. *Costume and Clothes* (Legacies series). New York: Thomson Learning, 1995.

INDEX